Contents

About This Book 4

Alphabet Recognition and Rhyme
A to Z Wrap 8
Alphabet Walk 11
A to Z Carpet Board 13
Magnetic Cookie Sheet 14
Alphabet Soup 16
Pick-and-Pull Rhymes 20

Consonants, Clusters, and Digraphs
Egg Carton Consonant Game 24
Cereal Box Consonant Search 25
File-Folder Football 26
Musical Paper Plates 30
Phonics Puzzles 31

Vowels
Flip the Flapjacks 34
Play Ball! 35
Phonics Fold-Ups 37
Pocket Chart Concentration 40
Sound Twister 41
Phonics-Shape Mini-Books 42

Word Blending
Bat the Ball! 47
Laundry Scoop Word Review 51
Cube of Sounds 52
Clown Slide 53

Phonics Review
Sound Jeopardy 55
Wheel of Practice 57
Beach Ball Toss 59
High-Five Shower Curtain 60
Sunny Syllables 62

About This Book

Phonics Games Kids Can't Resist!—No way, you say! Well, this book provides a variety of fun and engaging games, manipulatives, and activities that can be used to teach and reinforce phonics. All the activities chosen for this book are tried and true; I use them in my classroom on a regular basis. With games and activities such as Flip the Flapjacks and File-Folder Football, I am able to address the various learning styles of the children in my class to help them succeed at reading.

As you know, young children often find it difficult to sit still for long periods of time and complete worksheets. Therefore, I develop activities that will get them actively involved in learning. When developing activities, I try to find something that will be hands-on, fun, and out of the ordinary. I am constantly searching for new ideas—the "in" craze or something unusual to convert into teaching games. I never know when I might see something that will trigger an idea. I then incorporate it into a teaching activity. This helps children develop a positive attitude toward learning, and they learn while having fun.

The games, manipulatives, and activities presented in this book can be used in a variety of ways. From individual assessment to large group participation, the activities provide positive motivation for children to achieve. Also, once a skill is mastered, another skill can be incorporated into the same game format to provide learning games throughout the year with little additional effort or time.

—*Michelle K. Ramsey*

Helpful Hints

The following hints are provided to help you incorporate the games and activities into your classroom routine. Remember that phonics should be taught and reinforced on a daily basis. What better way than to provide the children in your class with a variety of hands-on games and activities.

★ Establish a designated area in your classroom for a phonics learning center. I suggest mounting a large pegboard on a wall. Purchase peg hooks and rings. Hole punch all your flashcards, game boards, and other materials to hang on the board. Small plastic baskets can be hung on the hooks to hold game pieces and smaller items. This provides easy access to all children, and all your phonics games and activities are located in one convenient place. Children can get a game during independent work or center time.

★ Another way to display game boards and other materials is to use the plastic ring holders found on canned drinks. Using yarn, tie the holders together to form a large sheet. Suspend the sheet from the ceiling and clip game boards and other materials to it with clothespins.

★ Make a set of flash cards for letters, sound-spellings, or words being taught. Place numbers on the back of each flash card. Correspond the number to the level of difficulty of the phonics skill. Children can use different levels of cards to increase the game challenge.

⭐ To make patterns, trace the outline of a picture using white tissue paper. Place the tissue paper on construction paper, posterboard, or a shower curtain. Trace over the pencil markings with a permanent marker. You will now have an outline of the pattern. Trace the outline with a marker. Color and laminate.

⭐ Using an overhead projector or photocopier, enlarge the game boards and cards to the size you need. To use the overhead, place a clear overhead sheet on the pattern. Using an overhead marker, trace the pattern. Place the pattern on the overhead and project it onto a large sheet of paper or tagboard taped to the wall. Trace the projected pattern on the paper or tagboard, cut, and decorate as desired.

⭐ Photocopy the game boards and cards on card stock to ensure durability.

⭐ To make the games more attractive and appealing, decorate the game boards with stickers, use shape-scissors to cut the edges of game pieces, or paste the game boards on colored construction paper or file folders.

⭐ Game pieces can be as creative as the game board. Use beanbags, small stuffed animals, plastic figures (cowboys, superhero action figures, soldiers), prize toys from food chains, and so on.

⭐ Remember, the games and activities provided can be used with individuals, small groups, or large groups. Many of them can be used for assessment. For example, a child can play a game or participate in an activity while you observe and assess what the child knows. Most important, choose games that reflect your instructional goals, meet child needs, and make learning fun. Enjoy!

Home-School Connections

A child's home environment is important to the success a child experiences in school. Parents and family members can be one of the greatest assets in ensuring that a child reads at home and practices key reading skills. There are three main ways to help make strong home–school connections using the games and activities presented in this book.

1. Conduct a parent make-and-take workshop. During the workshop, present the different activities parents can use to reinforce the skills you are teaching. Provide time for parents to laminate the games they make. Children can also participate in the workshop.

2. During the week, have each child make a game or activity to take home. Provide a step-by-step demonstration. Then allow children to create the games during independent or center time.

3. Make additional games and activities to send home with children. Or allow parents to check out games from you.

Remember, the games and activities you send home should be an extension of the day's activities. Send home only games that reinforce the skills a child needs. Be sure to include simple activity instructions with each game.

Resources

For further reading on phonics, see these classroom reference books:

⭐ *Phonics from A to Z: A Practical Guide* by Wiley Blevins (Scholastic, 1998)
⭐ *Phonics for the Teacher of Reading* by Marion Hull (Merrill, 1994)
⭐ *Phonics That Works!* by Janiel Wagstaff (Scholastic, 1994)
⭐ *Phonics They Use: Words for Reading and Writing* by Patricia Cunningham (HarperCollins, 1995)
⭐ *Teaching and Assessing Phonics: Why, What, When, How* by Jeanne Chall and Helen Popp (Educators Publishing Service, 1996)

A to Z Wrap

Players: 1

Skill

alphabet recognition

✶· Materials ·✶

- game boards, pages 9–10
- posterboard
- scissors
- glue or tape
- hole punch
- yarn

Phonics Fact

Alphabet recognition is a powerful predictor of early reading success. It is the speed and auto-maticity with which children can recognize letters, both in and out of order, that is critical. Slow letter recognition can hinder a child dur-ing phonics instruction, when the child is con-necting a specific letter to a specific sound.

Getting Ready

✶ Photocopy the game boards for Game 1.

✶ Attach Side 1 to the front of a same-size piece of posterboard, and Side 2 to the back. Make sure the sides are aligned. Cut and laminate.

✶ Cut a notch beside each letter using scissors. Cut a hole above the letter A using a hole punch.

✶ Thread a piece of yarn through the hole above the letter A and tie a knot to secure it.

How to Play

1 The player wraps the yarn in the notches in alphabet-ical order.

2 The player must state the letter name and correspon-ding sound.

3 When completed, the player self-checks by using the answer key on Side 2.

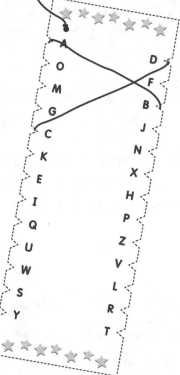

■·●·✶· Variation ·■·✶·●

Photocopy and enlarge the game boards for Game 2 and prepare as described above. In this game, children match upper- and lowercase letters.

A to Z Wrap
Game 1

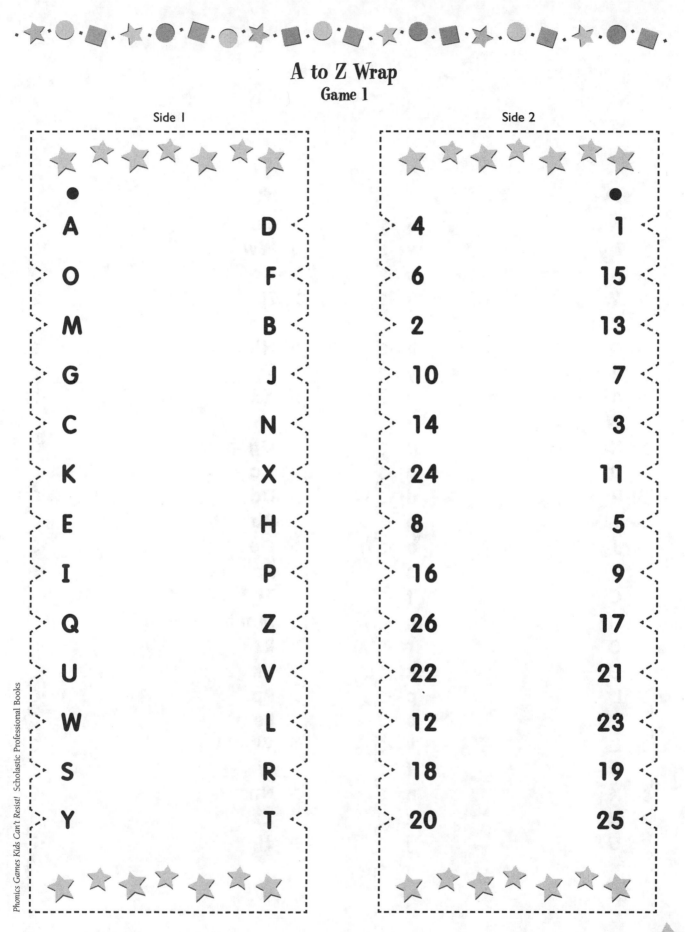

Side 1

A	D
O	F
M	B
G	J
C	N
K	X
E	H
I	P
Q	Z
U	V
W	L
S	R
Y	T

Side 2

4	1
6	15
2	13
10	7
14	3
24	11
8	5
16	9
26	17
22	21
12	23
18	19
20	25

Phonics Games Kids Can't Resist! Scholastic Professional Books

9

A to Z Wrap
Game 2

Side 1

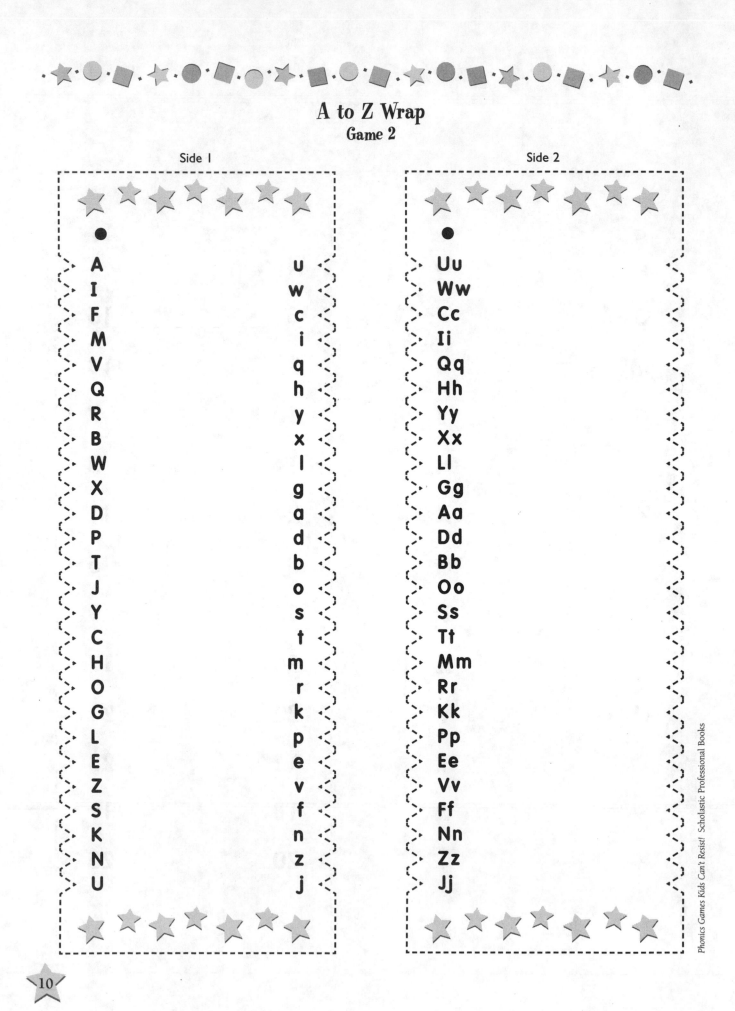

A
I
F
M
V
Q
R
B
W
X
D
P
T
J
Y
C
H
O
G
L
E
Z
S
K
N
U

u
w
c
i
q
h
y
x
l
g
a
d
b
o
s
t
m
r
k
p
e
v
f
n
z
j

Side 2

Uu
Ww
Cc
Ii
Qq
Hh
Yy
Xx
Ll
Gg
Aa
Dd
Bb
Oo
Ss
Tt
Mm
Rr
Kk
Pp
Ee
Vv
Ff
Nn
Zz
Jj

Phonics Games Kids Can't Resist! Scholastic Professional Books

Alphabet Walk

Players: 2 to 6

Skill

alphabet recognition

✦· Materials ·✦

- shower curtain
- permanent black marker

  optional:
- tagboard
- masking tape
- number cube pattern, page 12
- scissors
- tape

Getting Ready

✦ Write the letters of the alphabet in random order on the shower curtain, creating a path such as the one shown below. (Variation: Write the letters on large pieces of tagboard using a thick black marker. Laminate and tape the letters to the floor to create an alphabet path.)

How to Play

1 Children walk the alphabet path as they say each letter's name.

2 On a second walk, children say the sound that each letter stands for.

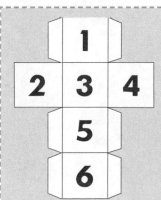

■·●·✦· Variation ·■·✦·●

| 1 |
| 2 3 4 |
| 5 |
| 6 |

Copy the number cube pattern and program as shown. Then cut out the pattern along the dotted lines, fold on the solid lines, and tape together. Have each child roll a number cube and walk the number of spaces indicated. Then the child must say the letter's name, the sound it stands for, and a word that begins with that sound-spelling.

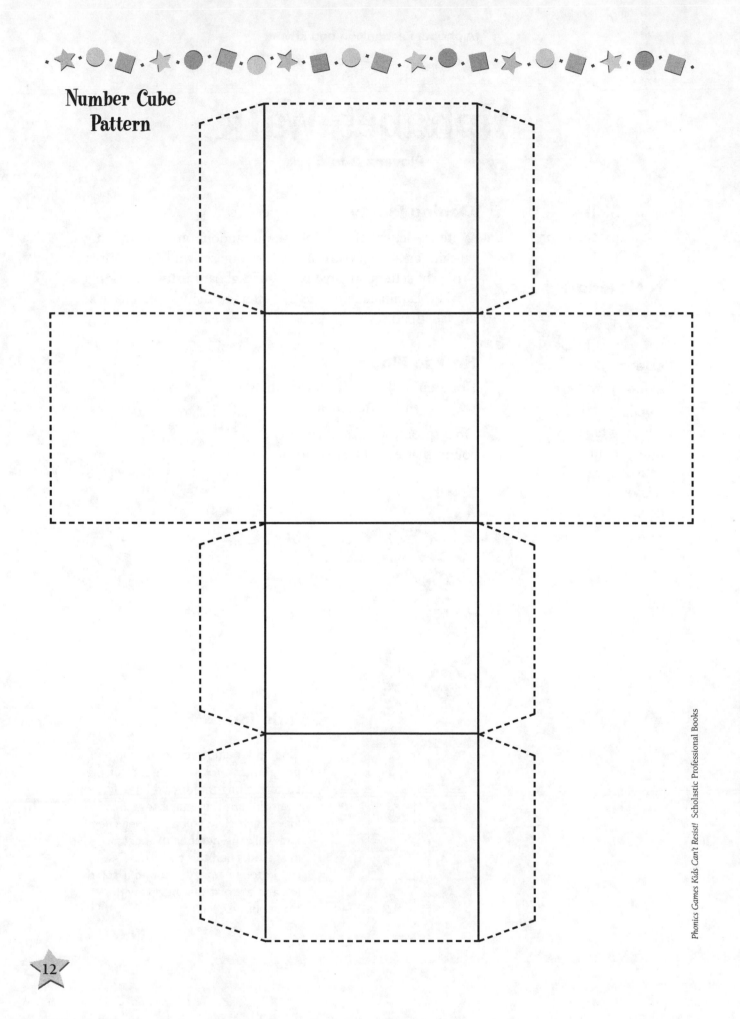

Number Cube
Pattern

Phonics Games Kids Can't Resist! Scholastic Professional Books

A to Z Carpet Board

Players: 1 to 3

Skill

alphabetical order

✦ Materials ✦

- carpet sample board (carpet stores often will donate old ones)
- fabric paint and brushes

Phonics Fact

Alphabet books are a natural and enjoyable way to develop children's alphabet recognition, teach that letters represent sounds, and build vocabulary. Fill your classroom with alphabet books. Select, read, and revisit a new alphabet book each week

Getting Ready

⭐ Remove the carpet samples from the carpet sample board. (Each board will have seven carpet samples across and four down, a total of 28 carpet samples.)

⭐ Write an alphabet letter on each carpet sample, using fabric paint.

How to Play

1 Each player begins with the top row and from left to right arranges the letters in alphabetical order by placing one carpet sample on each space.

2 When finished, the player states each letter's name and corresponding sound.

3 Players may wish to remove the carpet samples, use them as letter cards, and form as many words as possible. Suggest that they record the words formed on a separate sheet of paper.

Magnetic Cookie Sheet

Players: 2

Skill

alphabet recognition

✷· Materials ·✷

- steel cookie sheet
- magnetic alphabet letters

✷· Materials ·✷

- coconut tree pattern, page 15
- green and brown markers or crayons
- scissors
- glue
- steel cookie sheet
- set of magnetic alphabet letters
- *Chicka Chicka Boom Boom* by Bill Martin Jr. and John Archambault (Simon and Schuster Books for Young Readers, 1989) or an alphabet book of your choice

Activity 1

Getting Ready

★ Place the cookie sheet and magnetic letters in a learning center.

How to Play

1 One player places each letter on the cookie sheet as he or she states the sound the letter stands for. The player's partner checks each answer.

2 When completed, players switch roles.

Activity 2

Getting Ready

★ Photocopy and cut out the coconut tree pattern. Use green and brown markers or crayons to color the trunk, leaves, and coconuts.

★ Glue or tape the tree to the cookie sheet.

How to Play

1 Give each child half of the alphabet letters.

2 Read aloud the alphabet book *Chicka Chicka Boom Boom*. While you read the first part of the book, children place their letters on the cookie sheet as the letters' names are read. During the second part, children remove their letters from the cookie sheet.

3 When children become familiar with the letter names, read the book using the corresponding sound for each letter. For example, /a/ told /b/ and /b/ told /c/ and so on. Children place each letter on the cookie sheet tree when they hear the sound the letter stands for.

Coconut Tree Pattern

Alphabet Soup

Players: 1 to 6

Skill

alphabet recognition

· Materials · ·

- alphabet letters, pages 17–19
- construction paper
- scissors
- cooking pot
- large wooden spoon or ladle

Phonics Fact

Research shows that the two best predictors of early reading success are alphabet recognition and phonemic awareness. These two prerequisite skills are critical if children are to make sense of phonics instruction.

Getting Ready

★ Photocopy the alphabet letters and cut them out along the dotted lines.

★ Paste them to colored construction paper, laminate, and cut to create letter cards.

How to Play

1 Distribute the letter cards to children.

2 Each child in turn places a letter in the pot as he or she states the sound the letter stands for.

3 Stir the letters in the pot. Have volunteers pull one letter out of the pot, state the letter's name and corresponding sound, and name words that begin with the sound-spelling.

■ ● · ★ · Variation · ■ · ★ · ●

Instead of letter cards, use alphabet noodles. Have children wash their hands before handling the letters. After the activity, cook and serve real alphabet soup!

Alphabet Soup Letters

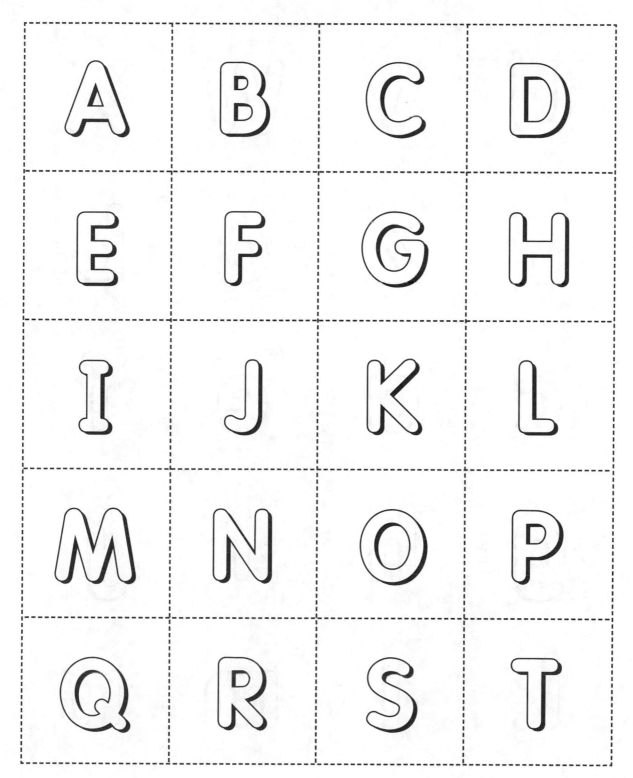

Alphabet Soup Letters

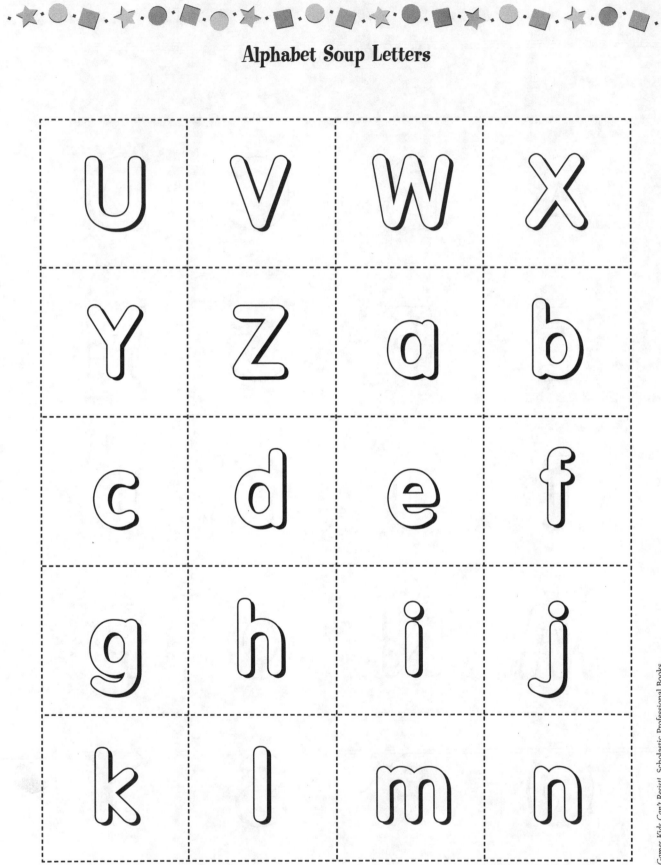

U	V	W	X
Y	Z	a	b
c	d	e	f
g	h	i	j
k	l	m	n

Phonics Games Kids Can't Resist! Scholastic Professional Books

Alphabet Soup Letters

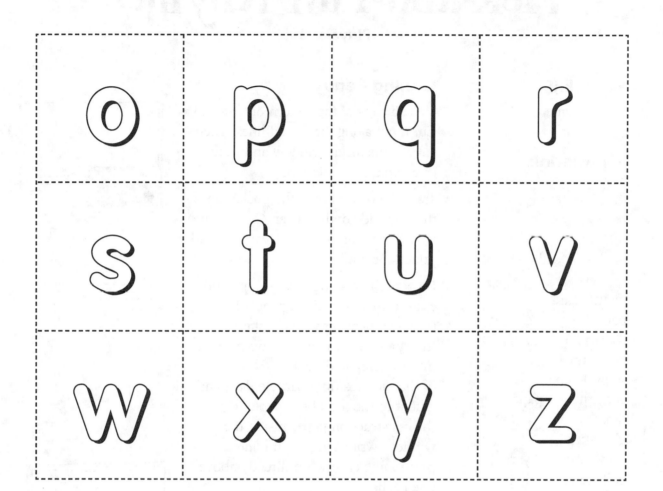

Pick-and-Pull Rhymes

Players: 2

Skill

rhyme

✦ Materials · ★

- folder pattern, page 23
- scissors
- file folder with pockets
- picture cards, page 22
- X-acto knife
- hole punch
- 9- by 12-inch construction paper
- tape
- glue stick
- 2-foot piece of yarn
- golf tee or bobby pin

Getting Ready

⭐ Make a copy of the pattern on page 23. Cut it out along the dotted lines. Then cut out the inside window and punch three holes, as indicated.

⭐ Trace the pattern onto the pocket on the right side of the folder. Cut out the large notch and the inside window and punch three holes.

⭐ Prepare the playing cards. Copy and cut out the pictures on page 22. (Enlarge them first, if you like.) Insert a sheet of construction paper into the prepared pocket. Choose one of the pictures (for example, *hat*) and glue it to the top of the paper. On the construction paper inside the window, write *hot*, *sat*, and *ham*, positioning each word directly above one of the holes.

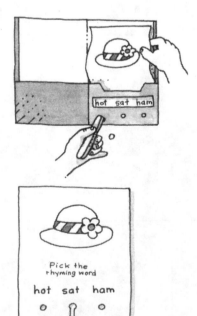

⭐ With the construction paper still inserted in the pocket, punch three holes in the paper. (The holes in the paper and in the pocket should line up.)

⭐ In the notched area, write *Pick the rhyming word*.

⭐ Remove the sheet of paper and enlarge the punched hole directly under the word *sat* until you've cut through the bottom of the paper, as shown.

★ Prepare the remaining picture cards using the remaining pictures and word sets.(See the chart below.)

sled	fish	boat
slide, bed, slab	dish, fog, fit	broke, tote, bet
frog	**bell**	**house**
log, fruit, few	ball, bet, well	how, mouse, mow
bone	**bus**	**tree**
boat, book, phone	fuss, bug, best	try, big, sea
pig	**nest**	**wheel**
wig, sag, pup	nice, best, neck	steal, will, what
sock	**cake**	**bike**
soon, knock, sunk	snip, snack, snake	lick, bite, hike

★ Punch a hole in the upper right-hand corner of the folder. Knot one end of the yarn through the hole. Wrap the other end around the tee and tape securely.

★ Insert the picture cards in the left-hand pocket of the folder.

How to Play

1 Have children play in pairs. One child chooses a picture card and places it in the right-hand pocket.

2 The other child says the name of each picture, reads each set of words, and chooses the word that rhymes with the name of the picture. To self-check, the child inserts the golf tee into the hole beneath the chosen word and tries to gently pull out the picture card. If the answer is correct, the picture card will slide out of the pocket. If the answer is incorrect, the card will remain in place.

■ ● ✦ Variations ■ ✦ ●

- Use the pictures on pages 43–46 to prepare additional playing cards.

- Use stickers or pictures from old workbooks to prepare picture cards that focus on beginning and ending clusters and digraphs. See example, left.

Pick-and-Pull Rhymes
Picture Cards

Pick-and-Pull Rhymes
Folder Pattern

Write skill or question in this area.

Write the three answer choices in this area.
Be sure to line up answers with the punched holes.

Egg Carton Consonant Game

Players: 1 or 2

Skill

consonants

✵ Materials ✵

- 2 egg cartons
- round stickers
- marker
- plastic counters

Getting Ready

⭐ Write the following spellings on round stickers. Place one sticker in each egg carton cup.

Game 1 (consonants): *b, c, d, f, g, h, j, k, l, m, n, p*

Game 2 (consonants): *q, r, s, t, v, w, x, y, z, m, f, l*

How to Play

1 Each player in turn places one counter in the egg carton, closes the lid, and shakes.

2 The player then opens the lid and identifies the spelling on which the counter landed and states the sound for which the spellings stands. One point is earned for each correct response. For an extra point, the player must state a word containing the sound-spelling.

3 Play continues until one player earns 20 points.

■•●•✵• Variations •■•✵•●

Prepare additional egg cartons so that children can practice other phonics skills, such as consonant digraphs and clusters or vowels.

Game 3 (consonant digraphs and clusters): *ch, sh, th, wh, ph, sl, st, br, fr, cl, sp, gl*

Game 4 (vowels): *a, e, i, o, u, ee, ea, ay, ai, oa, ow, igh*

Game 5 (vowels): *ou, ow, oo, oi, oy, ay, ea, oa, y, ie, igh, ew*

Cereal Box Consonant Search

Players: whole class

Skill

consonants/
consonant clusters

✦ Materials ✦

- empty cereal, food, and game boxes
- pencil and paper

How to Play

1 Distribute empty cereal, food, and game boxes to children.

2 Ask children questions related to phonics skills you are focusing on. For example, "Find all the words with /b/ as in *ball*." "Find all the words that begin with /bl/ as in *blue*."

3 Children must find the answers in the print on the boxes. To do this activity, children might enjoy working with partners or in small groups.

4 Help children use the words they find to create word walls related to each phonics skill. Invite children to add to the word wall as they encounter new words on packages, signs, and other reading sources.

■ ● ✦ Variation ■ ✦ ●

Place the boxes in a learning center. Write questions on index cards and tape them to each box. Expand the game to include other phonics skills. For example, "Find a word with three syllables," or "Find all the words with the long-*a* sound."

File-Folder Football

Players: 2 to 6

Skill

initial and ending
consonants

✦· Materials ·✦

- football field game
  board, pages 28–29
- scissors
- file folder
- glue stick
- game cards, page 27
- colored counters
  (2 colors)
- permanent marker

Getting Ready

⭐ Photocopy the game board patterns, cut them out, and glue the
two halves to the inside of a file folder.

⭐ Photocopy the game cards, laminate, then cut them out. On each
card write a word with the consonants you wish to review. For
initial and ending consonants you may wish to use these words:

initial consonants: *box, cookie, duck, fun, gate, hill, jam, king, lamp,
mitten, nine, park, queen, radio, soap, tell, vest, was, yarn*

ending consonants: *web, mud, leaf, rag, bell, Sam, ten, lip, jar,
dress, net, hive, fox*

How to Play

1 Divide the class into two teams. Each team selects a color
counter to serve as its football (or copy and color two extra
football patterns). Determine which end zone will represent the
touchdown for each team.

2 Place the football game cards on the 50-yard line. Place the
football counter for each team on the 10-yard line nearest the
opposing team's end zone.

3 In turn, one player from each team selects a game card, reads
aloud the word, and uses it in a sentence. For each correct
response, the team advances the "football" counter 5 yards
toward the end zone. For each incorrect answer, the team is
penalized and must move the football back 5 yards. The first
team to reach the end zone and make a touchdown wins.

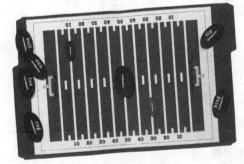

■·●·✦· Variations ·■·✦·●

Follow the instructions below to prepare larger versions of the
football game board. Adjust the size of the football field and
football patterns to the size of the game board you are using.

Posterboard Game: Cut a large green posterboard in half,
horizontally. Draw the football-field game board on the poster.

Shower Curtain Game: Use a permanent marker to draw the
football-field game board on a shower curtain.

File-Folder Football
Game Cards

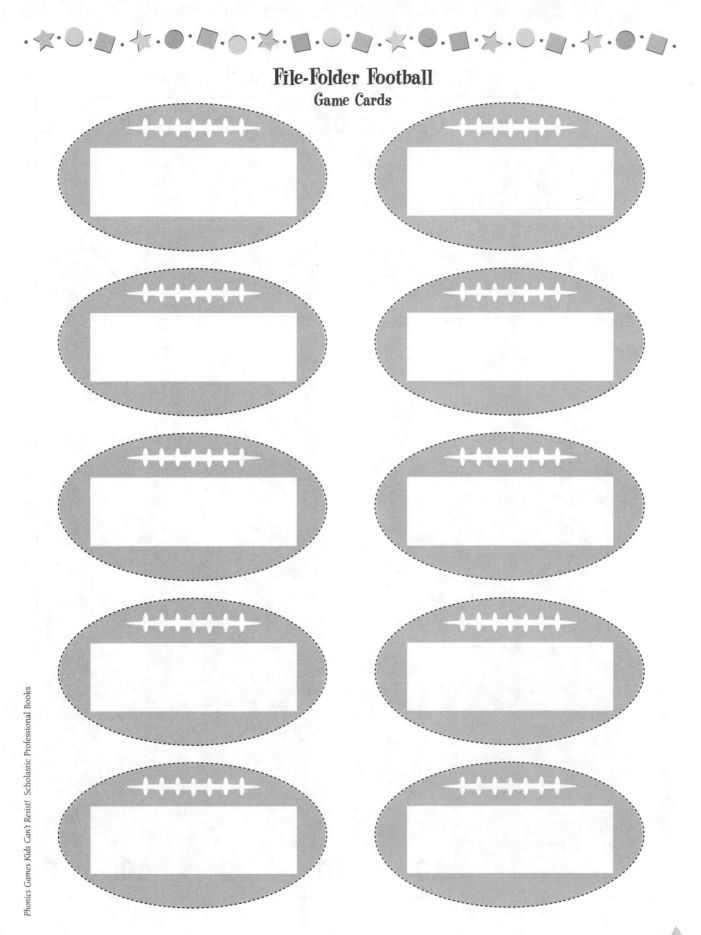

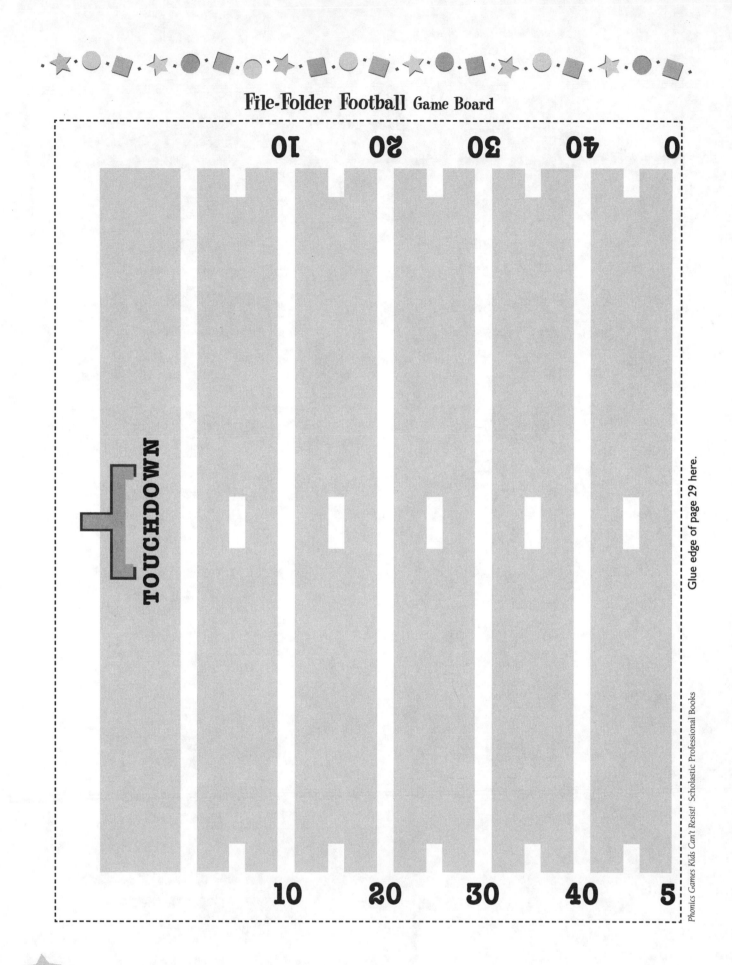

File-Folder Football Game Board

TOUCHDOWN

10 20 30 40 5

Glue edge of page 29 here.

File-Folder Football Game Board

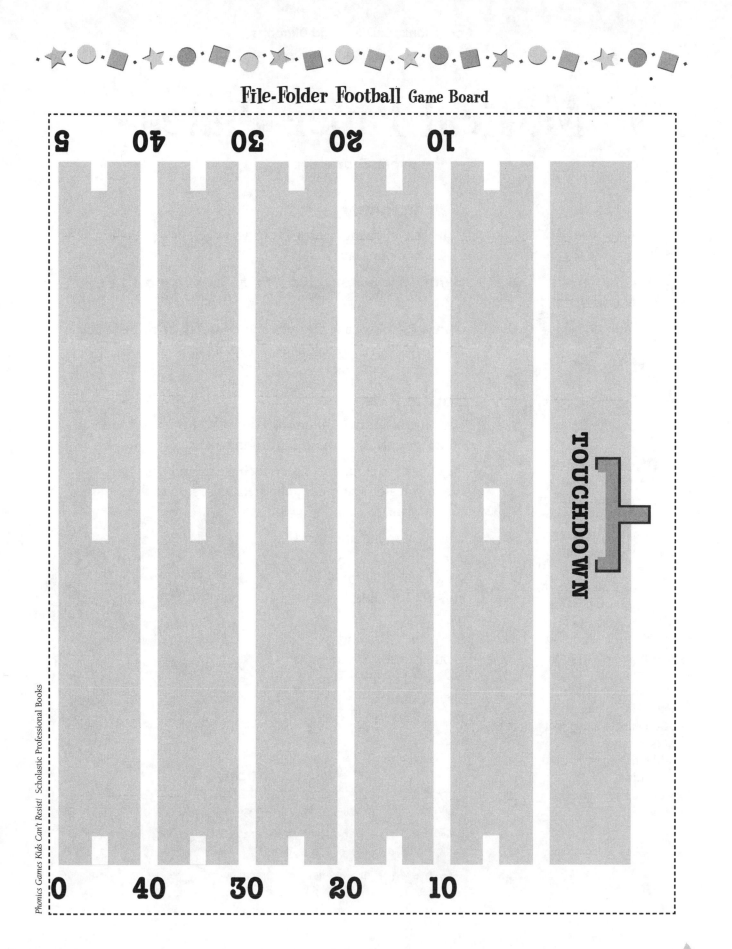

Musical Paper Plates

Players: 5 or more

Skill

consonants/
clusters and digraphs

✦ Materials ✦

- paper plates
- marker
- tape or CD player
- audiocassette or CD

Phonics Fact

A consonant digraph is a combination of two consonant letters representing a single consonant sound. The digraphs include *ch, th, sh, wh, ck, gh, ng,* and *ph*. A consonant cluster (or blend) is a combination of two or more consonants in which the sounds of both letters are blended and heard. Consonant clusters include *r*-blends (*br, gr, pr*), *l*-blends (*bl, cl, fl*), and *s*-blends (*sm, sn, st*).

Getting Ready

★ Write the following consonant or vowel spellings on the paper plates, one per plate:

Game 1 (consonants): *b, c, d, f, g, h, j, k, l, m, n, p, q, r, s, t, v, w, x, y, z*

Game 2 (consonant digraphs and clusters): *ch, sh, th, wh, thr, shr, ph, ck, br, fr, gr, tr, cl, fl, pl, sk, sm, sp, str, spr*

How to Play

1 Place the plates face up on the floor in a circle. Use the same number of plates as there are children.

2 Play music as children walk in a circle around the plates. When you stop the music, children must stop in front of the closest plate.

3 Call out a sound and word. For example, ask, "Who is standing in front of /f/ as in *fish*?" The child beside the "f" paper plate steps inside the circle and names another word that contains the sound-spelling. Then play continues.

■ ● ✦ Variations ■ ✦ ●

Write the following vowel spellings on paper plates, one per plate:

Game 3 (short and long vowels): *a, e, i, o, u, ai, ay, y, ee, ea, ie, igh, ow, oa, oe, a_e, i_e, o_e, e_e, u_e*

Game 4 (other vowels): *er, ir, ur, au, aw, oi, oy, ou, ow, oo, ew, ue*

Phonics Puzzles

Players: 1 or 2

Skill

consonants/consonant digraphs and clusters

✦ Materials ✦

- puzzle patterns, pages 32–33
- lightweight cardboard
- glue
- crayons (optional)
- scissors
- manila envelopes

Getting Ready

✦ Make multiple copies of the puzzle pattern pages. Glue them to lightweight cardboard for added durability. Color and laminate, if desired. Cut out the puzzle pieces and place each set in a manila envelope.

How to Play

1 Give each child or pair of children a set of puzzle pieces.

2 Let children work individually or with partners to complete the puzzle.

3 Once the puzzle is complete, ask children to say the sound that each spelling stands for and state a word that contains that sound-spelling.

▪ ● ✦ Variations ▪ ✦ ●

To make large, phonics floor puzzles, copy the letters and letter combinations from the puzzle pattern pages onto large sheets of posterboard. Be sure to leave space between the spellings. (As an alternative, write a word using each spelling and underline the spelling to highlight it.) Laminate, if desired. Separate the spellings by cutting the posterboard into puzzle pieces, one spelling per piece. You may wish to place an adhesive, such as Funtak, on the back of each piece to help hold it in place when the puzzle is put together. Place the puzzle pieces on the floor or a large table and play as directed above.

Make puzzles for children to practice other skills. For the sight-word puzzles, children must use each word in a sentence.

Puzzle 1 (sight words): *the, of, and, a, to, in, is, you, that, it, he, for, was, on, are, but, what, all, were, when*

Puzzle 2 (sight words): *we, there, can, your, which, their, said, if, do, has, more, her, like, see, could, no, little, after, where, does*

Puzzle 3 (short vowels): *a, e, i, o, u*

Puzzle 4 (long vowels): *ai, ay, y, ee, ea, ie, igh, ow, oa, oe, a_e, i_e, o_e, e_e, u_e*

Puzzle 5 (other vowels): *er, ir, ur, au, aw, oi, oy, ou, ow, oo, ew, ue*

31

Consonant Puzzle

Consonant, Digraph, and Cluster Puzzle

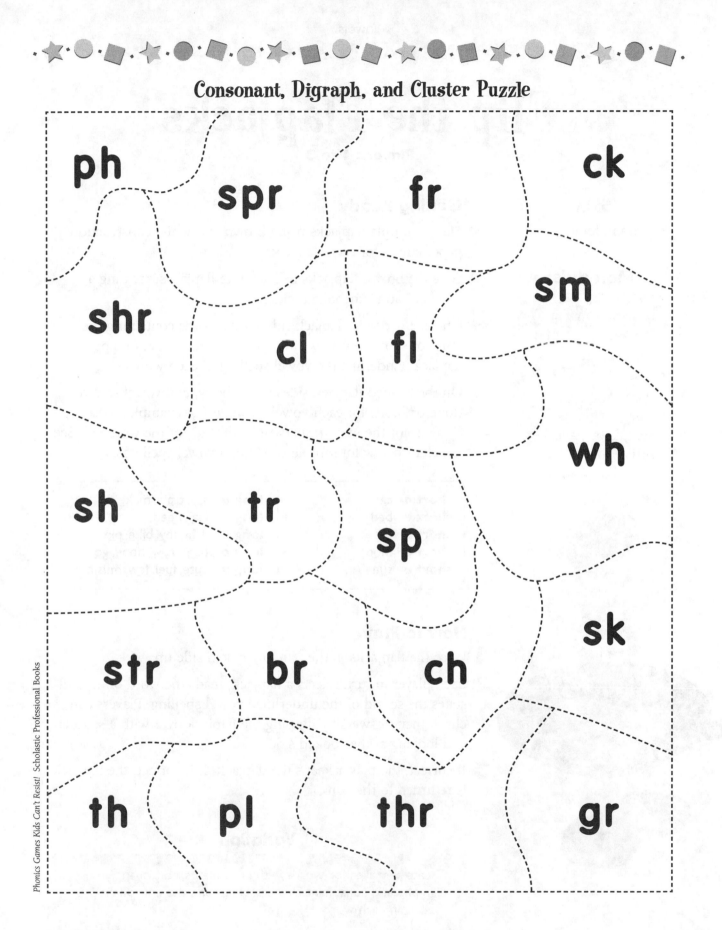

Flip the Flapjacks

Players: 1 to 3

Skill

short and long vowels

✴ · Materials · ✴

- 3-inch brown and white construction paper circles
- glue
- marker
- small frying pan
- spatula or pancake turner

Getting Ready

★ Make multiple flapjacks using brown and white construction paper circles for each flapjack.

★ Glue the brown flapjacks to the white flapjacks, creating a "cooked" and "uncooked" side.

★ On the uncooked flapjack sides write words containing the long- or short-vowel spellings you wish to review, one per flapjack. Underline the vowel spelling in each word.

★ On the cooked flapjack sides write the type of vowel sound (long or short) for each vowel spelling. For example, write "long *a*" for the word *train*; write "short *a*" for the word *cat*. See the chart below for sample words and vowel spellings.

short *a*	c<u>a</u>t	**long *a***	s<u>ay</u>, tr<u>ai</u>n, m<u>a</u>k<u>e</u>
short *e*	b<u>e</u>d	**long *e***	l<u>ea</u>f, n<u>ee</u>d,
short *i*	p<u>i</u>g	**long *i***	l<u>igh</u>t, m<u>y</u>, b<u>i</u>k<u>e</u>, p<u>ie</u>
short *o*	m<u>o</u>p	**long *o***	b<u>oa</u>t, r<u>ow</u>, h<u>o</u>p<u>e</u>, g<u>o</u>
short *u*	s<u>u</u>n	**long *u***	c<u>u</u>t<u>e</u>, f<u>ue</u>l, f<u>ew</u>, m<u>u</u>sic

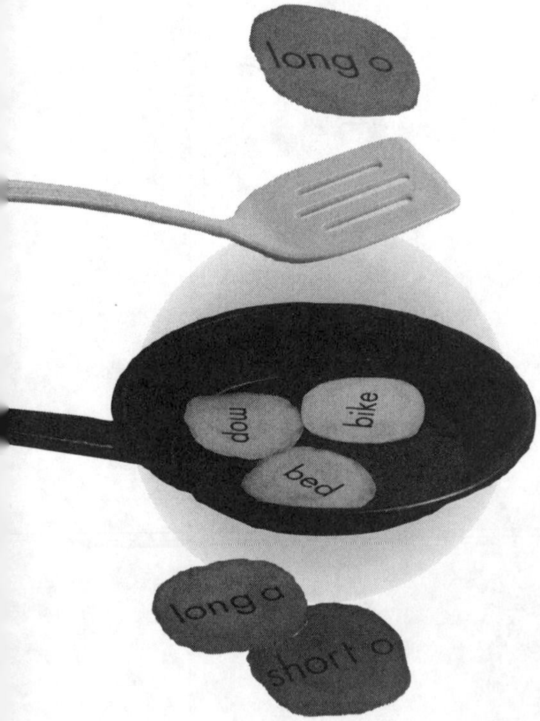

How to Play

1 Place the flapjacks in the pan, uncooked side up.

2 Each player in turn selects a flapjack, reads the word on it, and states the sound of the underlined vowel spelling. Players can check their answers by flipping the flapjack over with a spatula and looking at the cooked side.

3 If correct, the player keeps the flapjack. If incorrect, the flapjack is returned to the pan.

■ · ● · ✴ · Variation · ■ · ✴ · ●

Create pancakes for words with consonants, consonant digraphs, and consonant clusters. Underline the consonant spelling in each word.

Play Ball!

Players: 2 teams

Skill

vowels

★ · Materials · ★

- baseball game patterns, page 36
- file folder
- scissors
- glue or tape
- marker
- crayons

Phonics Fact

The category of other vowels includes *r*-controlled vowels (*ar, er, ir, or, ur*), diphthongs (*oi, oy, ou, ow*), and variant vowels (*oo*).

Getting Ready

★ Photocopy the pattern page. Cut out the two baseballs and the game board. Paste the game board to the inside of a file folder.

★ Make multiple copies of the bat patterns and cut them out. Write the following words on the bats, one per bat:

Game 1 (short vowels): *cat, can, bat, flash, that, bell, best, check, smell, when, fish, hill, miss, trick, stick, lock, mop, frog, spot, mom, duck, bug, buzz, skunk, run*

Game 2 (long vowels): *cake, train, say, skate, face, feet, queen, each, baby, niece, bike, dry, child, pie, flight, boat, rope, go, sold, below, cube, music, cute, few, rescue*

Game 3 (other vowels): *chair, care, pear, bird, turtle, better, card, garden, start, born, chalk, small, laundry, thaw, boy, noise, house, allow, proud, moon, blue, grew, duty, book, cookie*

★ On the back of each bat, write a number between 1 and 4. This will indicate the number of bases the player can move. Only use the number 4 two times, the number 3 three times.

How to Play

1 Divide the class into two teams. Invite children to name their teams using words with long and short vowels, for example, "The Short-*A* Batters."

2 Each team colors a baseball to serve as a marker.

3 In turn, one player on the first team selects a bat-word card and reads aloud the word. If the word is correctly read, the player moves the baseball the number of bases indicated on the back of the card. If the player is incorrect, the team earns an out.

4 When three outs are earned, the second team is up at bat.

5 You may wish to have partners "bat" together so that more proficient readers can help struggling readers.

Play Ball! Game Board

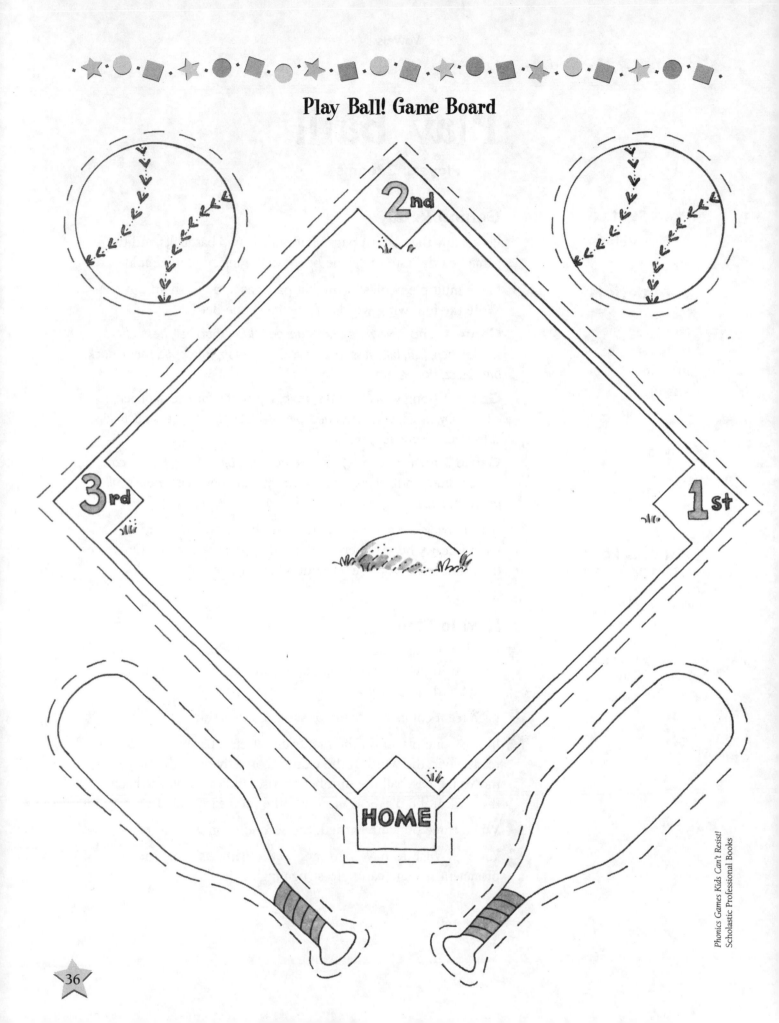

2nd

3rd

1st

HOME

Phonics Games Kids Can't Resist!
Scholastic Professional Books

Phonics Fold-Ups

Players: 1

Skill

vowels

✦ Materials ✦

- large unlined index cards
- markers

Phonics Fact

To help children focus on vowel sounds and spellings, use minimal contrasts. For example, have children read word pairs in which only the vowel spelling is different, such as *hat/hit, rid/ride, bat/boat.* Then provide sentence completion exercises with answer choices varying only in the vowel spelling. For example, *I ____ the ball. (hat, hot, hit)*

Getting Ready

✦ Fold each index card as shown to create game cards.

✦ Write a word on the front of the game card and underline the vowel spelling. Write the type of vowel sound (long or short) on the inside of the card. Focus on words with the vowel spellings you wish to review. Sample words for each vowel spelling are provided in the chart below. Additional words, including those for other vowel sounds, can be found on pages 38 and 39.

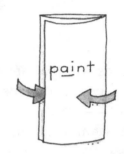

Outside of Card	Inside of Card	Outside of Card	Inside of Card
cat	short *a*	light	long *i*
bed	short *e*	my	long *i*
pig	short *i*	bike	long *i*
mop	short *o*	pie	long *i*
sun	short *u*		
		boat	long *o*
say	long *a*	row	long *o*
train	long *a*	hope	long *o*
make	long *a*	go	long *o*
leaf	long *e*	cute	long *u*
need	long *e*	fuel	long *u*
		few	long *u*
		music	long *u*

How to Play

1 Invite children to read the word on the card and state the vowel sound.

2 Children can self-correct by opening the card "doors."

■·●·✦· Variation ·■·✦·●

Encourage children to create their own cards. Place blank index cards and sample completed cards in a learning center. Children can use the cards to quiz classmates.

Short- and Long-Vowel Word Lists

Words with /ă/: am, as, at, back, bad, bag, band, bat, bath, black, can, cap, cat, catch, clap, class, crack, crash, dad, fan, fast, fat, flag, flat, glad, glass, grab, had, ham, hand, has, hat, lamp, land, last, mad, man, map, mat, math, pass, past, path, plan, plant, quack, ran, rap, rat, sack, sad, sand, sat, stamp, stand, tap, that, track, trap, van

Words with /ĕ/: bed, bell, best, bet, cent, check, desk, dress, egg, end, fell, get, help, jet, left, leg, let, men, mess, met, neck, nest, net, pen, pet, red, rest, sell, sent, shell, sled, smell, spell, spend, step, tell, ten, test, them, then, web, well, went, wet, when, yes

Words with /ĭ/: big, bill, bit, brick, chin, clip, did, dig, dish, fill, fish, fit, fix, gift, hid, hill, him, his, hit, in, is, it, kick, lift, list, miss, mitt, mix, pick, pig, rip, ship, sit, six, skin, skip, stick, swim, thin, this, trick, trip, which, wig, will, win, wish, zip

Words with /ŏ/: block, box, chop, clock, cloth, dog, doll, dot, drop, fox, frog, got, hop, hot, job, knock, lock, log, lot, mom, mop, moth, not, on, ox, plot, pond, pop, pot, rock, shock, shot, shop, sock, spot, top

Words with /ŭ/: brush, bug, bump, bunch, bus, but, buzz, club, crust, cup, cut, drum, duck, dug, dump, dust, fun, gum, hug, hunt, hut, jug, jump, just, luck, much, mud, must, nut, plug, plum, plus, pump, rub, rug, run, rush, rust, shut, skunk, such, sun, truck, trunk, up, us

Words with /ā/: bake, brake, brave, cage, cake, came, chase, date, face, game, gate, gave, grade, grape, lake, late, made, make, name, page, place, race, same, save, shape, skate, space, take, vase, wave, whale, brain, chain, mail, main, nail, paid, pail, pain, paint, rain, sail, snail, stain, train, wait, clay, day, gray, hay, may, pay, play, say, stay, way

Words with /ē/: be, me, we, bee, cheese, deep, feed, feel, feet, green, keep, knee, meet, need, see, seed, beach, bean, beat, cheap, clean, dream, each, eat, heat, lead, meal, neat, leaf, any, baby, candy, city, daisy, dusty, easy, lady, many, brief, chief, cities, field, niece

Words with /ī/: bike, bite, dime, drive, fine, five, hide, ice, kite, life, like, line, mice, mile, nice, nine, ride, shine, side, size, slide, time, white, wide, wife, by, cry, dry, fly, my, sky, why, blind, child, find, kind, wild, die, pie, tie, bright, fight, high, light, might, night, right

Words with /ō/: cold, go, gold, hold, no, old, so, sold, told, bone, broke, hole, home, hope, joke, nose, note, phone, rope, rose, stone, those, vote, whole, wrote, boat, coach, coat, goat, loaf, road, soap, throat, toad, blow, flow, grow, know, show, slow, snow, throw, window, yellow, goes, toe

Words with /yōō/: cube, cute, huge, mule, use, bugle, future, human, menu, museum, music, pupil, regular, unit, usual, few, preview, review, view, argue, continue, fuel, rescue, value, beautiful, beauty

Words with /ŏŏ/: book, brook, cook, foot, good, hood, hook, look, shook, stood, took, wood

Words with /ōō/: boot, broom, cool, food, goose, groom, hoop, hoot, kangaroo, loose, moo, mood, moon, moose, noon, roof, room, school, scoop, shampoo, smooth, soon, spoon, too, tooth, zoo, zoom, blue, clue, due, glue, true, blew, chew, crew, drew, flew, grew, knew, new, flute, rude, rule, tune, duty, truth, tuna

Words with /ô/: salt, chalk, talk, walk, all, ball, call, fall, small, tall, wall, because, caught, daughter, launch, laundry, pause, sauce, taught, awful, claw, crawl, draw, jaw, law, lawn, raw, saw, straw, yawn

Words with /oi/: avoid, boil, choice, coin, join, moist, noise, oil, point, poison, soil, spoil, voice, annoy, boy, cowboy, destroy, enjoy, joy, loyal, royal, soy, toy, voyage

Words with /ou/: about, bounce, cloud, count, found, ground, house, loud, mouse, mouth, noun, ouch, out, pound, proud, round, shout, sound, south, allow, brown, clown, cow, crowd, crown, down, gown, growl, how, now, owl, plow, powder, power, towel, tower, town, wow

Words with /âr/: air, chair, fair, hair, pair, care, dare, hare, rare, scare, share, spare, square, stare, bear, pear, wear

Words with /ûr/: burn, curb, curl, curve, fur, hurt, nurse, purple, purse, Thursday, turkey, turn, turtle, bird, birth, circle, circus, dirt, first, girl, shirt, stir, third, thirst, after, better, certain, clerk, ever, fern, germ, her, letter, mother, nerve, other, over, person, river, sister, under, verb, water, winter

Words with /är/: arm, art, artist, bark, barn, car, card, cart, charge, chart, dark, far, farm, garden, hard, jar, large, march, mark, park, part, shark, sharp, smart, spark, star, start, yard

Pocket Chart Concentration

Players: 2 to 6

Skill

vowels

✦ Materials ✦

- 50 small, unlined index cards (25 of one color, 25 of another color)
- marker
- pocket chart

Getting Ready

⭐ Write the numbers 1 to 25 on index cards of one color, one number per card. On the index cards of the other color, write the following words and vowel spellings, one per card:

Game 1 (short vowels): *extra turn; short a, cat; short e, ten; short i, pig; short o, mop; short u, bug; short a, sand; short e, smell; short i, trick; short o, sock; short u, shut; short a, fast; short i, swim*

Game 2 (long vowels): *extra turn; ai, train; ay, gray; ee, seed; ea, neat; y, by; ie, pie; igh, sight; long o, go; oa, boat; ow, throw; oe, toes; ue, fuel*

⭐ Place the vowel spelling and word cards in the pocket chart in random order. See illustration 1.

⭐ On top of each vowel spelling or word card, place a number. See illustration 2.

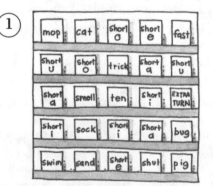

How to Play

1 Each player in turn calls a number. The "emcee" lifts the number so the child can see the word or vowel spelling underneath.

2 The player then chooses another number trying to make a word/vowel-spelling match (for example, the short *a-* and *cat* cards match). If a match is made, the player gets to keep the cards. If not, the next player takes a turn. The player who has the most matches at the end of the game wins.

Sound Twister

Players: 2 to 5

Skill

vowels

✦ Materials ✦

- Twister® game mat and spinner
- crasable marker

Getting Ready

✦ Write the following spellings on the game mat and spinner, one per circle or space. The spelling and color on the spinner should match that on the game mat.

Game 1:
Left Foot: *e, i, o, u*
Left Hand: *e, a, u, o*
Right Hand: *a, e, i, o*
Right Foot: *i, e, a, u*

Game 2:
Left Foot: *ai, ea, a_e, oo*
Left Hand: *ow, y, ie, aw*
Right Hand: *ay, ee, i_e, oi*
Right Foot: *oa, igh, o_e, ou*

How to Play

1 Place the game mat and spinner on the floor.

2 Play Sound Twister the same way as Twister®, with the following modifications:

- As each player spins, he or she must say the sound the spelling stands for and state a word containing that sound-spelling.

- The player then places his or her body part on the appropriate space as requested on the spinner.

Note: Since the spellings may be spread out, the player may have to be on just one space at a time.

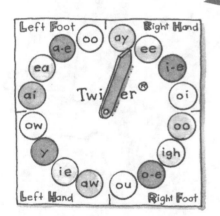

▪ ● ✦ Variations ✦ ▪ ● ●

Let children practice initial and ending consonant blends and digraphs with these versions of Sound Twister.

Game 3:
Left Foot: *th, sl, br, sh*
Left Hand: *ld, ck, str, shr*
Right Hand: *wh, ch, sm, ph*
Right Foot: *pr, tr, cl, ng*

Game 4:
Left Foot: *b, c, d, f*
Left Hand: *g, h, j, k*
Right Hand: *l, m, n, p*
Right Foot: *r, s, t, w*

Phonics-Shape Mini-Books

Players: whole class

Skill

vowels

✷· Materials ·✷

- phonics-shape patterns, pages 43–46
- scissors
- construction paper
- stapler
- markers or crayons

Phonics Fact

It is important for children to recognize the multiple spellings for each vowel sound. Begin a word wall in which you collect sample words for each vowel spelling. For example, under "long *a*," you might place the following word cards: *cake*, *train*, *play*. Refer to the word wall during reading and writing. Use the words on the wall to model how to sound out and spell words.

Getting Ready

✷ Make multiple copies of the phonics-shape patterns and cut them out.

✷ Also trace and cut out a cover for each book from a pattern cut from construction paper.

What to Do

1 Help children make mini-books using the patterns. Each child needs several copies of each pattern. Staple the copies of one pattern together to form a book with a construction paper cover on top.

2 Have children write words that contain the vowel sound in the pattern's name. For example, children write words with long-*a* spellings on each page of the train mini-book. For sounds with multiple spellings, such as long *a* (-*ai, -ay*), children can highlight the different spellings on each page using a different colored marker or create separate books for each spelling.

▪·●·✷· Variations ·▪·▪·✷·●

Help children make mini-books using the following shape patterns for sounds and spellings other than those provided on pages 43–46:

treasure chest (digraph *ch*)   shell (digraph *sh*)

thirty (digraph *th*)   whistle (digraph *wh*)

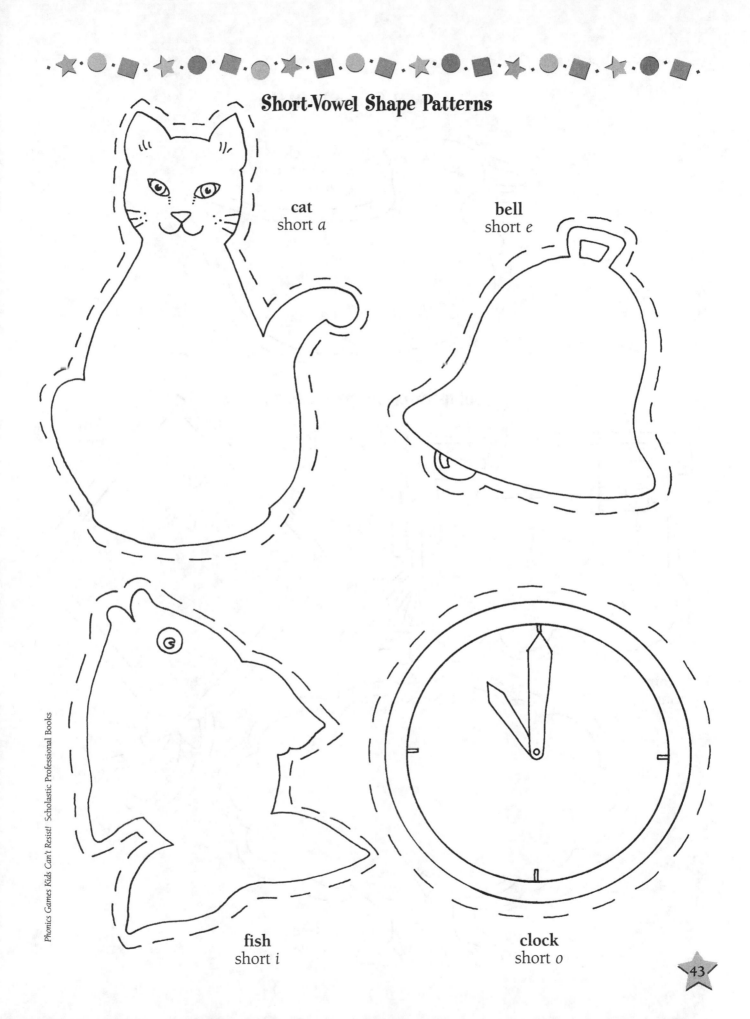

Short-Vowel Shape Patterns

cat
short *a*

bell
short *e*

fish
short *i*

clock
short *o*

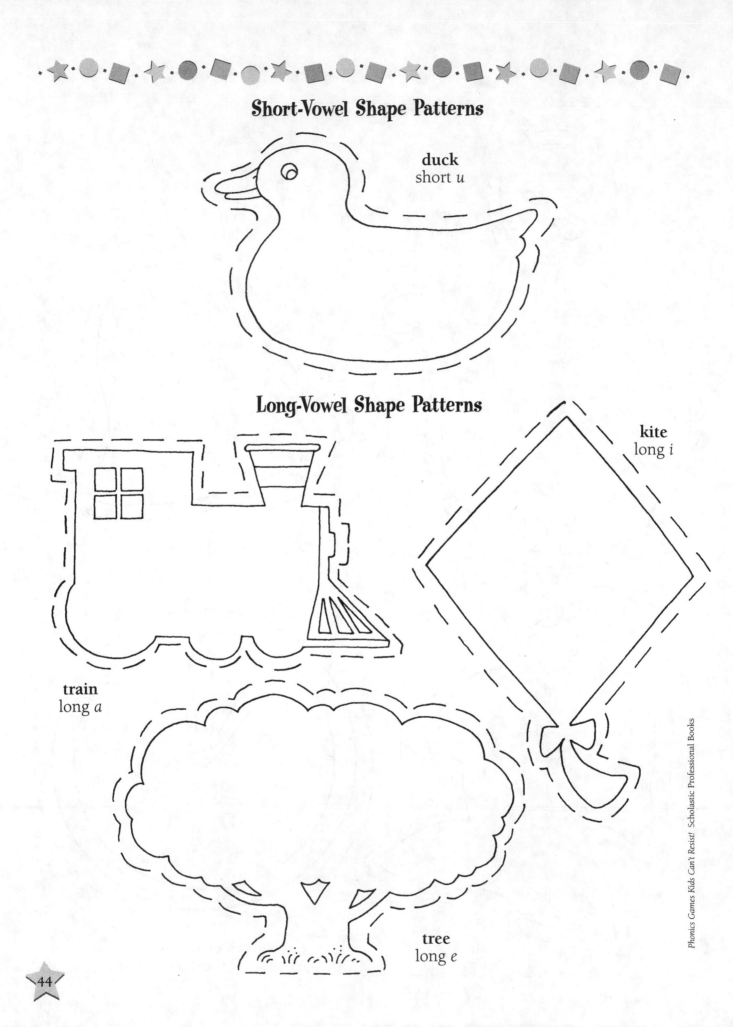

Short-Vowel Shape Patterns

duck
short *u*

Long-Vowel Shape Patterns

kite
long *i*

train
long *a*

tree
long *e*

Long-Vowel Shape Patterns

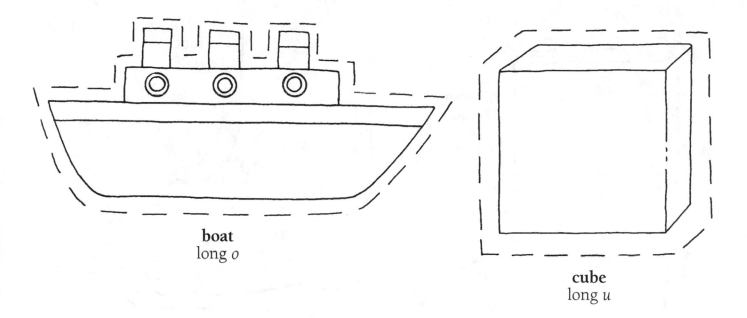

boat
long *o*

cube
long *u*

r-Controlled Vowel- and Variant-Vowel Shape Patterns

flower
/ou/

boy
/oi/

r-Controlled Vowel- and Variant-Vowel Shape Patterns

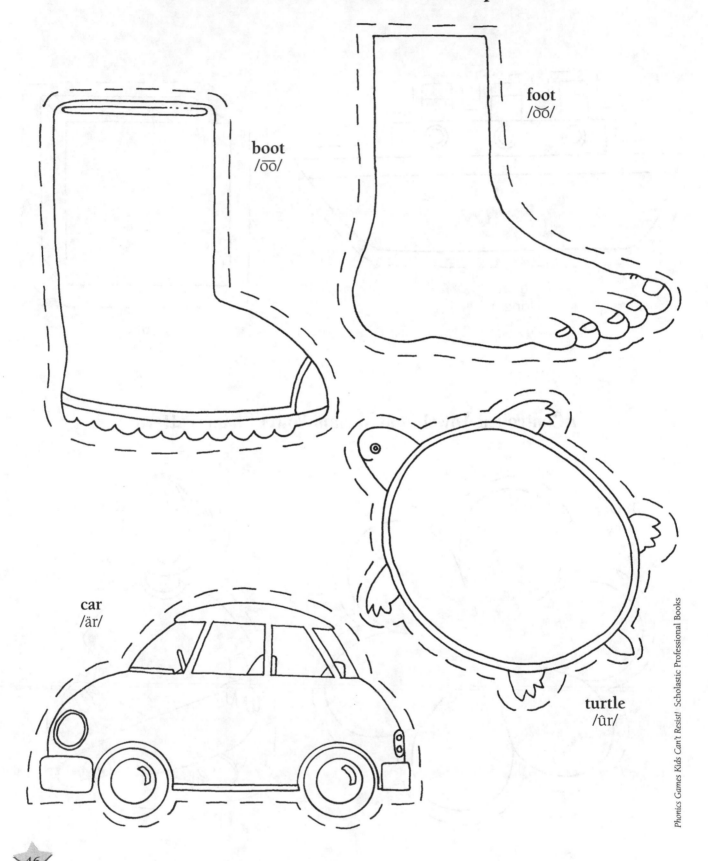

foot
/o͝o/

boot
/o͞o/

car
/är/

turtle
/ûr/

Phonics Games Kids Can't Resist! Scholastic Professional Books

Bat the Ball!

Players: whole class

Skill

blending

✦ Materials ✦

- ball patterns, page 49
- bat patterns, page 50
- scissors
- marker

Phonics Fact

A phonogram (or word family) is a letter (or series of letters) that stands for a sound, syllable, or series of sounds without reference to meaning. For example, the phonogram *at* contains two letters and stands for two sounds (/ăt/). It can be found in words such as *at, cat,* and *Saturday*. The phonogram *oat* contains three letters and stands for two sounds (/ōt/). It can be found in words such as *boat, float,* and *oatmeal*.

Getting Ready

⭐ Make 30 balls using the ball pattern. On each ball, write one of the following consonant digraphs or clusters: *ch, sh, th, wh, ph, thr, shr, ph, br, cr, dr, fr, gr, pr, tr, bl, cl, fl, gl, pl, sl, sk, sm, sn, sp, st, sw, str, spr, spl.*

⭐ Make 10 bats using the bat pattern. On each bat, write one of the following sets of vowel phonograms: *ack, ail, ain, ake; ame, an, ank, ap; ash, at, ate, ay; eat, ell, est, ice; ick, ide, ight, ill; in, ine, ing, ink; ip, ock, op, uck; ig, unk, ale, aw; ir, oke, ore, ump; or, ang, oast, oom.* (For other phonograms, see page 48.)

⭐ Create a ball field in the classroom by designating one corner of the room for each base, including home plate.

How to Play

1 Divide the class into two teams. Invite children to name their teams using words that contain clusters and digraphs (for example, "The Great Base Stealers").

2 In turn, one player from the first team selects a bat. A pitcher "throws" a ball to the player. The player must then form a word using the beginning sound-spelling on the ball and one or more of the vowel spellings on the bat.

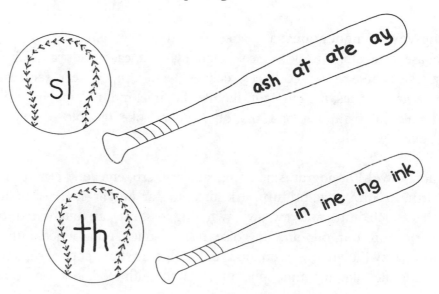

3 If the player can use all four vowel spellings to make a word, he or she earns a home run. If the player can use three of the spellings, a triple is earned. If two are used, a double is earned. And if one is used, a single is earned. If the player is unable to form a word, an out is earned.

4 The player moves that number of bases and the game continues. After three outs, the second team is up at bat.

▪·●·✦· Variations ·▪·✦·●

- You may wish to have teams take turns at bat. In this version, more than one player can be on any given base and teams earn points until three outs are scored.

- Use other vowel phonograms focusing on the vowel spellings you wish to review. See the lists of phonograms scored.

Vowel Phonograms

Short-Vowel Phonograms: ab, ack, act, ad, aft, ag, am, amp, an, ance, anch, and, ang, ank, ant, ap, ash, ask, asm, asp, ast, at, atch, ath, ax, ead, ealth, eath, eck, ed, edge, eft, eg, eld, elf, ell, elp, elt, em, en, ence, ench, end, ength, ense, ent, ep, ept, esh, ess, est, et, etch, ext, ib, ick, id, iff, ift, ig, ilk, ill, ilt, im, imp, in, ince, inch, ing, inge, ink, int, ip, is, ish, isk, isp, iss, ist, it, itch, ive, ix, ob, ock, od, oft, og, omp, ond, op, ot, otch, ough, ox, ome, on, ough, ove, ub, uch, uck, ud, udge, uff, ug, ulk, ull, um, umb, ump, un, unch, ung, unk, unt, up, us, ush, ust, ut, utch, utt

Long-Vowel Phonograms: ace, ade, age, aid, ail, ain, aint, aise, ait, ake, ale, ame, ane, ange, ape, ase, aste, ate, ave, ay, aze, eak, eigh, ey, e, ea, each, ead, eak, eal, eam, ean, eap, ear, ease, east, eat, eath, eave, ee, eech, eed, eek, eel, eem, een, eep, eer, eet, eeze, iece, ief, ield, ibe, ice, ide, ie, ied, ier, ies, ife, igh, ight, ike, ild, ile, ime, ind, ine, ipe, ire, ise, ite, ive, uy, y, ye, o, oach, oad, oak, oal, oam, oan, oast, oat, obe, ode, oe, oke, old, ole, oll, olt, ome, one, ope, ose, ost, ote, ove, ow, own

Other Vowel Phonograms: air, are, ear, earn, erb, erge, erk, erm, ern, erve, ir, ird, irk, irl, irst, irt, irth, ur, urb, urge, url, urn, urk, urse, urt, ar, ard, arge, ark, arm, arn, arp, art, all, alk, alt, aught, aunch, aunt, ault, aw, awl, awn, ong, oss, ost, oth, ought, oar, oor, orch, ord, ore, ork, orm, orn, ort, our, oil, oin, oint, oise, oist, oy, ouch, oud, ounce, ount, ound, our, ouse, out, outh, ow, owl, own, ew, o, oo, ood, oof, ool, oom, oon, oop, oose, oot, ooth, ooze, oup, ube, uce, ude, ue, uke, ule, ume, une, ure, use, ute, uth, ood, ook, oot, ould, ull, ush

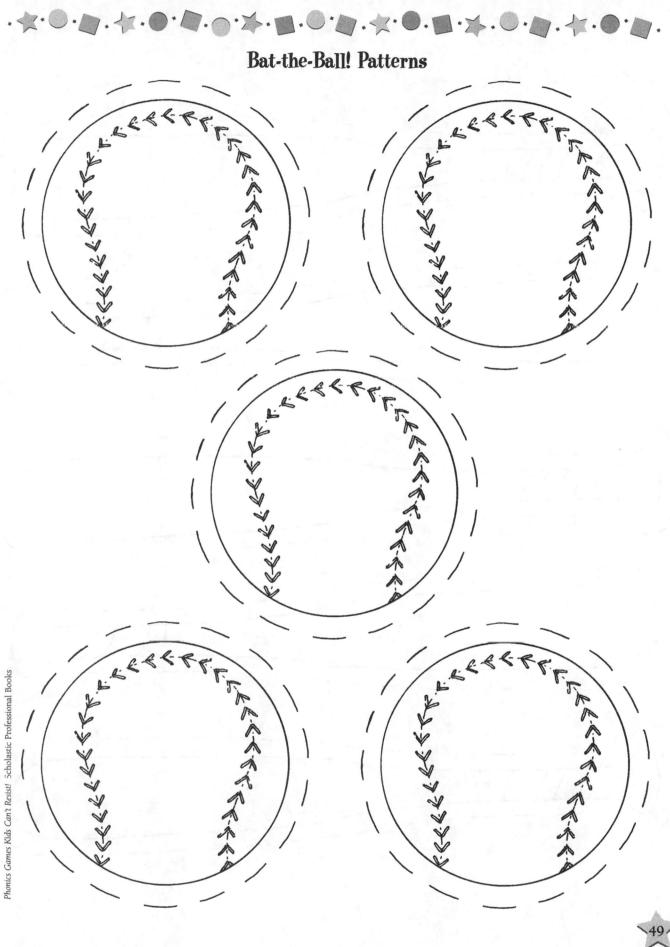

Bat-the-Ball! Patterns

Phonics Games Kids Can't Resist! Scholastic Professional Books

49

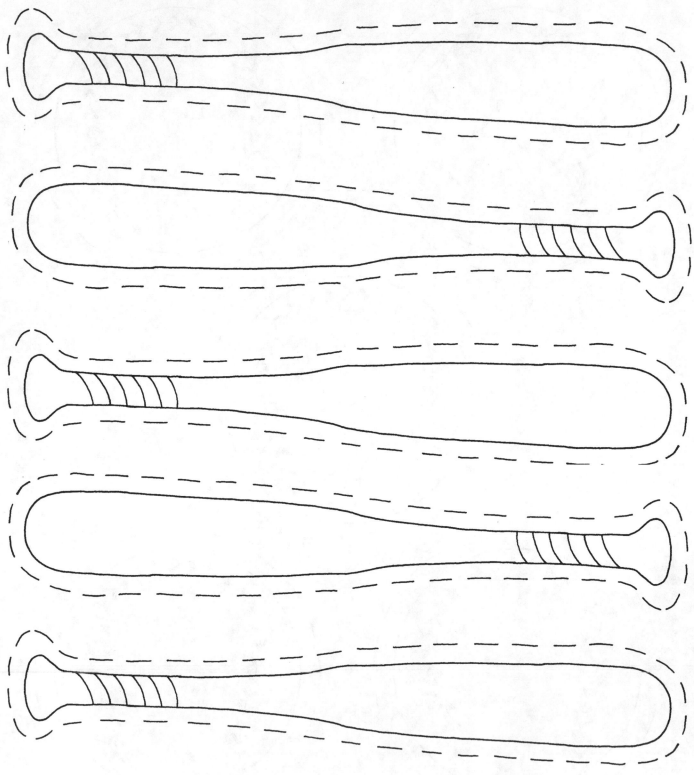

Bat-the-Ball! Patterns

Laundry Scoop Word Review

Players: 1 to 3

Skill

blending

✦· Materials ·✦

- 26 laundry scoops
- marker
- index cards

Phonics Fact

Blending is simply stringing together the sounds that make up a word. Research reveals that when teachers spend larger than average amounts of time modeling blending and providing their students with opportunities to blend words, the students in their classes show above-average gains on achievement tests. This is because modeling blending shows children how words "work" and helps them attach sounds to spellings.

Getting Ready

⭐ Write each letter of the alphabet on the inside or outside of the scoops, one per scoop.

⭐ Place the vowel scoops in one pile, the consonant scoops in another pile. Make a card label for each pile.

How to Play

1 Each player in turn selects one vowel and two consonant scoops.

2 If a word can be formed from the letters on the scoops, the player earns one point.

3 The player continues by placing another consonant scoop on top of the beginning or ending consonant scoop to try to form another word. (The scoops will nest one inside of the other.) After five points are earned, the next player takes a turn.

vowels   consonants

■·●·✦· Variation ·■·✦·●

Replace the vowel scoops (*a, e, i, o, u*) with more complex vowel spellings, such as *ai, igh, ee, ea, ou, oa, oi,* and *ow*.

Cube of Sounds

Players: 1 or 2

Skill

blending

✦· Materials ·✦

- 4 small, empty, washed milk cartons (or use cube pattern, page 12)
- scissors
- contact paper
- markers
- stickers or self-sticking notes
- paper and pencils

Getting Ready

⭐ Cut the tops off two equal-size milk cartons.

⭐ Invert one carton and place it inside the other to form a closed cube.

⭐ Cover the cube with contact paper.

⭐ Write a consonant or blend on each side of one cube. Write a vowel spelling on each side of the other cube.

⭐ Make new games by replacing the spellings on each cube with new spellings you wish to review. Use stickers or self-sticking notes.

Note: If milk cartons are not available, make multiple copies of the cube pattern. Write one spelling on each side. Then cut out the pattern along the dotted lines, fold on the solid lines, and tape together.

Game 1
Cube 1: *br, st, p, ch, sl, m*
Cube 2: *a, ou, ai, ee, igh, o*

Game 2
Cube 1: *cr, sn, r, sh, fl, b*
Cube 2: *e, ea, ow, oi, oo, ew*

Game 3
Cube 1: *dr, sp, h, th, l, d*
Cube 2: *i, u, ay, oo, oy, ie*

How to Play

1 Each player in turn rolls the two cubes and blends the sounds together. (Place the consonant cube first.)

2 The player then completes the word. For Example: If the player rolls *s* and *a*, the player can use this word-beginning (/sa/) to form the word *sat*.

3 The player then records the word and uses it in a sentence.

Clown Slide

Players: 2

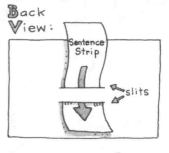

Skill

reading words

✴ Materials ✴

- clown pattern, page 54
- scissors
- posterboard
- glue stick or tape
- sentence strips
- markers
- X-acto knife

Phonics Fact

For maximum reading growth, children need to be reading text on their independent and instructional reading levels every day. The *independent reading level* is the level at which a child can read a text without help. Comprehension should average 90% or better, and word recognition should average 95% or better. The *instructional reading level* is the level at which a child reads the text with teacher guidance and is challenged enough to stimulate reading growth. Comprehension should average 75% or better, and word recognition should average 90% or better.

Getting Ready

✰ Photocopy, enlarge, and cut out the clown pattern. Color and mount onto posterboard.

✰ Use an X-acto knife to make slits along the dotted lines (for the sentence strips).

✰ Cut sentence strips and write words that contain the phonics skills you wish to review. See the word lists on pages 38–39.

How to Play

1 The first player reads each word as it passes through the clown's mouth. The player's partner checks for accuracy. Then the players switch turns.

2 Note: This activity can be used as an engaging way to assess children. Use the following word lists from the San Diego Quick Assessment (LaPray and Ross, 1969) to determine a child's reading level.

3 Write each word list on separate sentence strips. Have children read the word lists until they miss three or more words on one list. Two errors on a word list determine the child's instructional reading level. Three or more determine their frustration level; children should not be reading materials on this level for maximum reading growth to occur.

Preprimer: *see, play, me, at, run, go, and, look, can, here*

Primer: *you, come, not, with, jump, help, is, work, are, this*

Grade 1: *road, live, thank, when, bigger, now, always, night, spring, today*

Grade 2: *our, please, myself, town, early, send, wide, believe, quietly, carefully*

Grade 3: *city, middle, moment, frightened, exclaimed, several, lonely, drew, since, straight*

Grade 4: *decided, served, amazed, silent, wrecked, improved, certainly, entered, realized, interrupted*

Clown Pattern

Sound Jeopardy

Players: 2 to 6

Skill

phonics review

★· Materials ·★

- 45 unlined index cards (three different colors)
- marker
- pocket chart

Getting Ready

★ Make five each of $100, $200, $300, and $400 cards using the first color index cards.

Money Cards **5** each

★ Make five topic cards using the second color index cards. Label each topic card with one sound-spelling, such as *sh, ou,* or short *a*.

Topic Cards **1** each

★ Make twenty definition cards using the third color index cards, five cards per topic. On the back of each card write a word. These words should contain the sound-spellings listed on the topic cards. On the front of each card, write the word's definition.

20 Definition Cards

EXAMPLE

not small — Front (definition)

big — Back (answer)

★ Place one topic card at the top of each of five rows on the pocket chart.

★ Place the four definition cards for each topic under the topic card, one per row. The definitions should face forward. See illustration 1 below.

①

(front view of cards)   **(back view of cards)**

★ Place a money amount card on top of each definition card. See illustration 2.

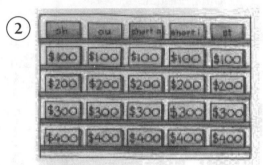

②

How to Play

1 Each player in turn chooses a topic and money amount. The "emcee" lifts the money card to reveal the definition.
Example:
Child: I would like short *i* for $100, please.
Definition: "not small"
Child: What is "big"?

2 If the player correctly identifies the word in the form of a question, he or she keeps the money card. If the player is incorrect, the card is returned to its original place. Play continues with the next player.

3 After the board is cleared, the player with the most money wins.

■·●·✦· **Variation** ·■·✦·●

Instead of a pocket chart, use a carpet sample board. (Floor covering stores will often donate old ones.) Each board will have 7 columns and 4 rows. Remove the carpet samples. Make topic cards, money cards, and definition cards to fit into the spaces.

Wheel of Practice

Players: 2 to 6

Skill

phonics review

✦ Materials ✦

- game board and spinner, page 58
- scissors
- brass fastener
- unlined index cards
- chalkboard or dry-erase board
- tagboard (optional)

Getting Ready

⭐ Photocopy the wheel game board and spinner. Color and laminate, if desired.

⭐ Attach the spinner to the center of the game board using a brass fastener. (You may wish to glue the spinner to tagboard for added durability and ease of spinning.)

⭐ Make definition cards using the index cards. On the front of each card write a word. These words can be words containing the sound-spellings you wish to review (see pages 38 and 39) or words from current science and social studies units. On the back of each card, write the word's definition.

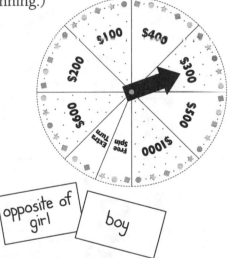

How to Play

1 This game is played like the popular television game, Wheel of Fortune™. Choose a definition card. Tell the players how many letters are in the word, draw that number of spaces on the chalkboard, and read aloud the definition.

2 The first player spins the wheel and gives a letter. If the letter is in the word, write the letter on the board and award the player the dollar amount. (It is best to keep score on the board for each player.)

3 Play continues until a player solves the puzzle.
Example:
The teacher writes on the board: _ _ _ _ _ _ _
The teacher says: "This means to talk quietly."
w h i s p e r

Note: If players guess the word from the definition alone, don't provide the definition prior to play. Instead, have the player who identifies the word provide a definition. Read the definition on the card to check for accuracy.

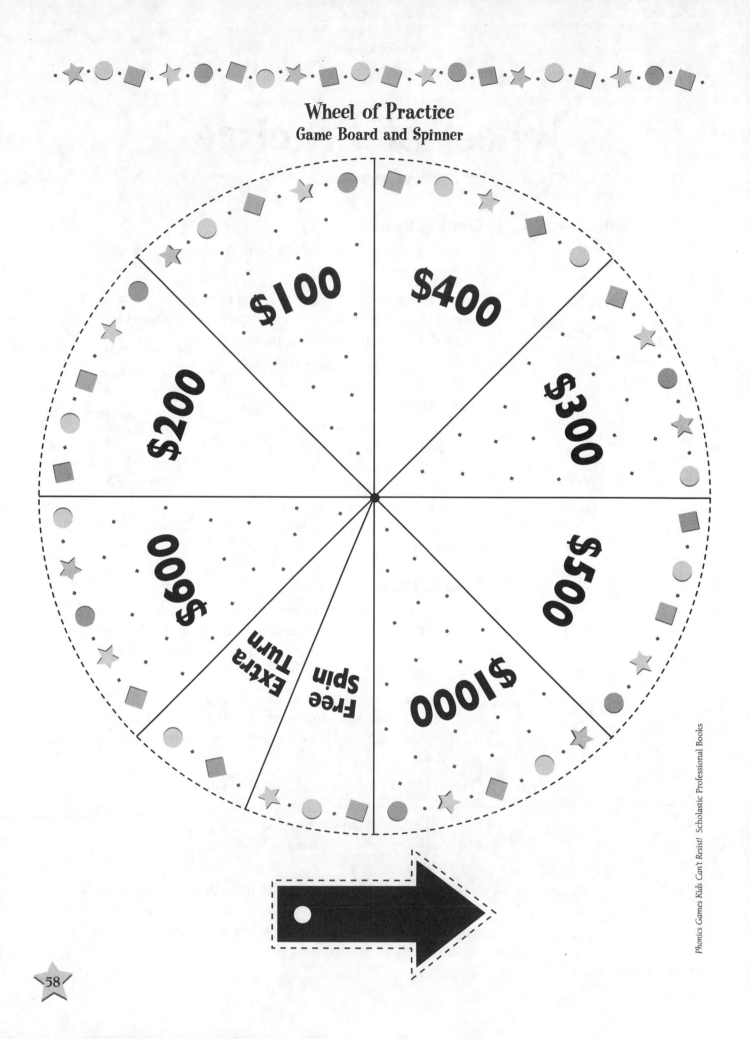

Wheel of Practice
Game Board and Spinner

$100

$400

$200

$300

$600

$500

Extra Turn

Free Spin

$1000

Phonics Games Kids Can't Resist! Scholastic Professional Books

Beach Ball Toss

Players: whole class

Skill

phonics review

✦· Materials ·✦

- plastic inflatable beach ball
- permanent marker

Getting Ready

★ Inflate a beach ball. With a permanent marker, randomly write any sound-spellings you wish to review.

How to Play

1 Have children stand in a circle. Toss or bounce the ball to a child.

2 The child says the sound for the spelling that is closest to his or her right-hand thumb.

3 The child then states a word containing that sound-spelling and uses the word in a sentence.

4 The child tosses or bounces the ball to another child. The game continues in this manner.

High-Five Shower Curtain

Players: 2 to 6

Skill

phonics review

✴ · Materials · ✴

- hand pattern, page 61
- scissors
- plastic shower curtain (solid color)
- permanent marker
- beanbag

Getting Ready

★ Photocopy and cut out the hand pattern. Randomly make multiple tracings of the hand pattern on a shower curtain with a permanent marker.

★ Write a sound-spelling on each hand. Use sound-spellings you wish to review, such as *a, ai, sh,* and *tr*. (Note: To create two games in one, write the letters *A* to *Z* on the front of the shower curtain and more complex sound-spellings on the back.)

★ Place the completed shower curtain on the floor.

How to Play

1 Have children stand 2 to 3 feet from the shower curtain, facing away from the curtain.

2 Each player in turn throws a beanbag over his or her shoulder. The child has to say the sound for the spelling the beanbag lands on or is closest to. The child then gives a word that contains that sound-spelling and uses the word in a sentence.

3 If the player tosses the beanbag off the shower curtain, he or she earns a strike. Three strikes and the player loses a turn.

4 If the beanbag lands on a hand the player has already landed on, he or she earns a ball. After earning four balls, the player chooses any sound-spelling.

5 After each correct response, the players give each other a "High Five" hand slap.

Hand Pattern

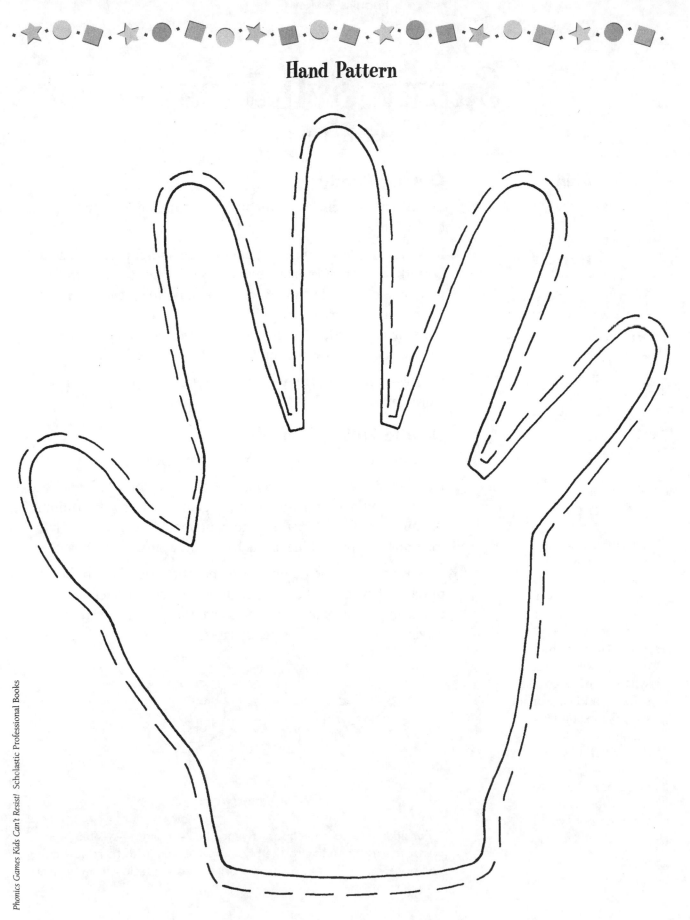

Sunny Syllables

Players: 1 or 2

Skill

syllabication

✴ Materials ✦

- sun patterns, page 63
- scissors
- poster board
- glue stick
- marker
- file folder
- pencil and paper

Phonics Fact

• • • • • • • • •

Instead of teaching a long list of syllabication rules, many of which are unreliable, focus your instruction on common syllable patterns. These include open syllables, closed syllables, prefixes and suffixes, and consonant + *le*. For example, explain to children that when they see the letters *le* at the end of a word, the consonant before it plus *le* form the last syllable, as in *table* or *handle*.

Getting Ready

⭐ Draw four large circles on the inside of a file folder. Number the circles *1* to *4*.

⭐ Make four copies of the sun pattern page and glue each page to posterboard. Then laminate and cut out the suns. On each sun, write one of the following words: *annoy, banana, remember, sing, listen, watch, happiness, football, little, thermometer, triangle, dinosaur, motorcycle, idea, stamp, reinvented, weight, tiger, phone, environment.* (Each word contains 1, 2, 3, or 4 syllables.)

⭐ On the back of the sun, write the number of syllables each word contains.

How to Play

1 Place the pile of suns face up on the game board.

2 Each player in turn selects a sun, reads aloud the word, and places it on the correct space on the game board by determining the number of syllables the word contains. Players can check their answers by looking at the back of the sun.

3 The player earns the number of points corresponding to the number of syllables the word contains for each correct answer. For example, the player would receive three points for the word *banana* since it contains three syllables.

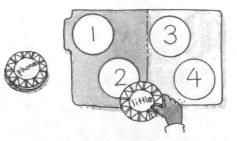

■ ● ✴ Variation ■ ✦ ●

For additional games, choose twenty 1-, 2-, 3-, and 4-syllable words corresponding to the phonics skills you wish to review or choose vocabulary words from current reading, science, and social studies units.

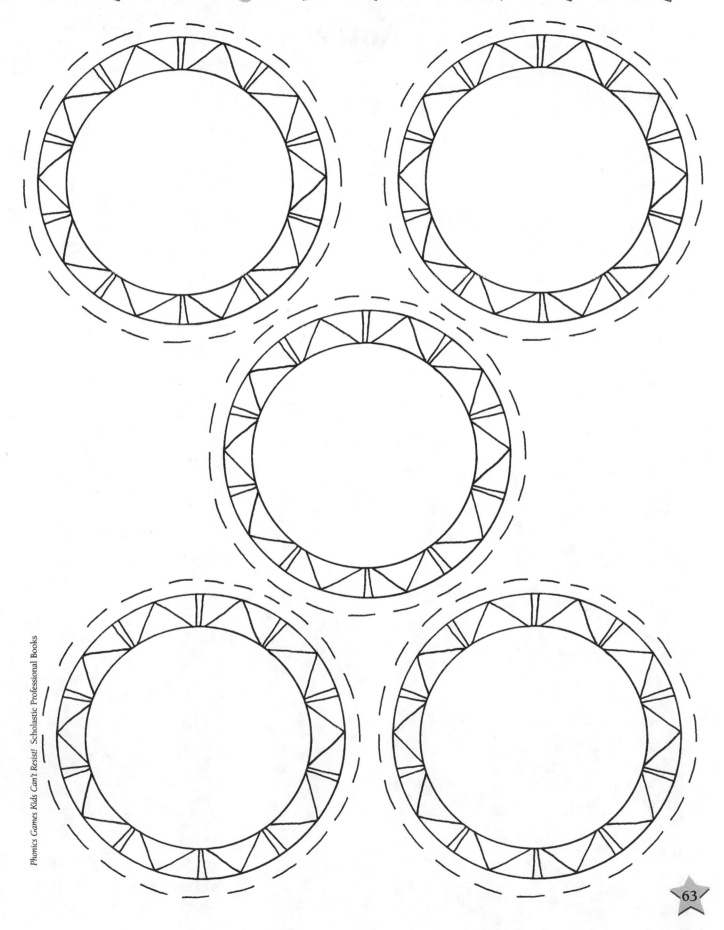

63

Notes